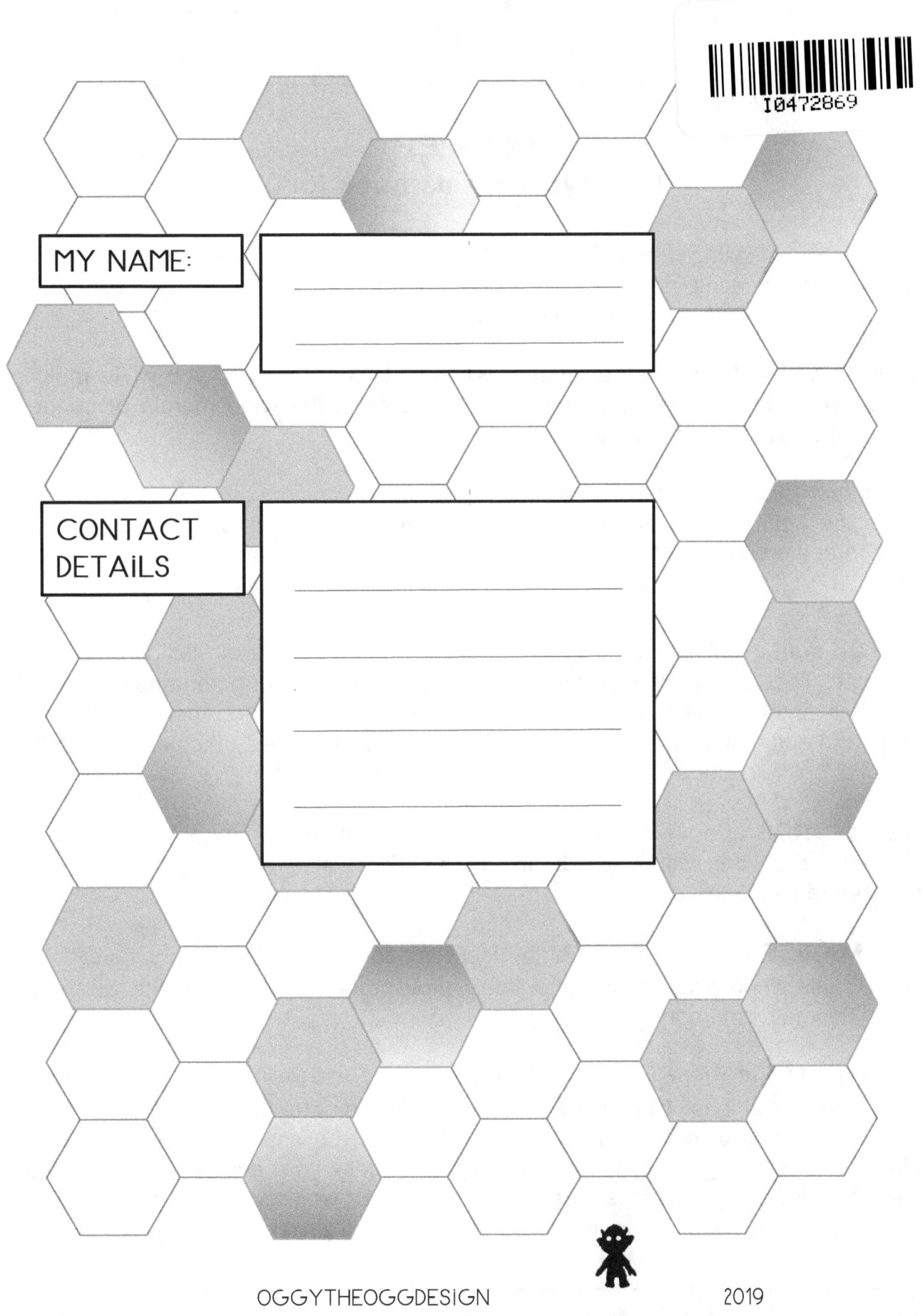

MY NAME:

CONTACT DETAILS

IN BRIEF
Who/What is this book for?

This system of taking notes (The Cornell System) is ideal for high school or college level students, adult note-takers, business meetings, conferences, presentation notes, minute taking and so many other things, too!

It allows you to keep track of questions/thoughts that occur to you while making notes. You can also go back and add comments in the wide margin or connect ideas between one source and another.

The paper is divided into **three areas**: A note-taking column (on the right) which is twice the size of the keyword column (on the left). There is also a summary section at the bottom of the page.

How do I use it?

NOTES from a lecture/meeting/book/DVD are written in the note-taking column on the right. They should contain the main ideas. <u>**Don't**</u> use long sentences; <u>**Do**</u> use abbreviations or even symbols. Record YOUR abbreviations on the Aide Memoire page and add to it as you go. Use Headings to show changes in topic, and number or bullet point key ideas. For your own sanity - write legibly!

KEY WORDS or possible test questions are written in the key points column on the left. Edit the notes as soon as possible after (or even during) the lecture/presentation.

SUMMARISE in your own words the facts and ideas in the summary space.. You can do this when revising or immediately after note-taking. **Speak** the words out loud. This helps memory.

STUDY - Take the time to revisit your Notes - at least 10 minutes for the next three days, then for at least 10 minutes a week. Cover the note-taking column, then look at the questions or cue-words column, and speak the answers to the questions, ideas, or facts <u>OUT LOUD</u> in your own words. Check your answers for immediate feedback. By studying a little bit each day and each week, you will have a greater success rate and retain more information. **Enjoy the process!**

CONTENTS

SUBJECT	TITLE	DATE	PAGE

CONTENTS

SUBJECT	TITLE	DATE	PAGE

CONTENTS

SUBJECT	TITLE	DATE	PAGE

CONTENTS

SUBJECT	TITLE	DATE	PAGE

Aide Memoire of Abbreviations

THIS IS NOT A DOODLE PAGE 🙂 DiAGRAMS/MiND-MAPS

Relates to Page: _____

Subject:

Title:

Date:

Key Points:

Notes:

Summary:

SAY OUT
LOUD
WHEN
REVISING

Page:	Subject:
Date:	Title:

Key Points:

Notes:

Summary:

SAY OUT
LOUD
WHEN
REVISING

Subject: 　　　　　　　　　　　　　　　Page:

Title: 　　　　　　　　　　　　　　　Date:

Key Points:

Notes:

Summary:

SAY OUT
LOUD
WHEN
REVISING

Relates to Page: _____

Subject:	Page:
Title:	Date:

Key Points:

Notes:

Summary:

SAY OUT
LOUD
WHEN
REVISING

Page:	Subject:
Date:	Title:

Key Points:

Notes:

Summary:

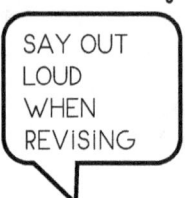

Subject:

Page:

Title:

Date:

Key Points:

Notes:

Summary:

SAY OUT
LOUD
WHEN
REVISING

Relates to Page: _____

Subject:	Page:
Title:	Date:

Key Points:

Notes:

Summary:

SAY OUT
LOUD
WHEN
REVISING

Page:	Subject:
Date:	Title:

Key Points:

Notes:

Summary:

Subject:

Page:

Title:

Date:

Key Points:

Notes:

Summary:

SAY OUT
LOUD
WHEN
REVISING

Relates to Page: _____

Subject:

Page:

Title:

Date:

Key Points:

Notes:

Summary:

SAY OUT
LOUD
WHEN
REVISING

Page:	Subject:
Date:	Title:

Key Points:

Notes:

Summary:

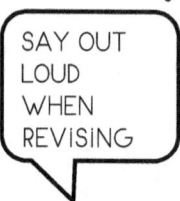

SAY OUT
LOUD
WHEN
REVISING

Subject:

Page:

Title:

Date:

Key Points:

Notes:

Summary:

SAY OUT
LOUD
WHEN
REVISING

THIS IS NOT A DOODLE PAGE 🙂 DIAGRAMS/MIND-MAPS

Relates to Page: _____

Subject:

Title:

Date:

Key Points:

Notes:

Summary:

SAY OUT
LOUD
WHEN
REVISING

Page:	Subject:
Date:	Title:

Key Points:

Notes:

Summary:

SAY OUT
LOUD
WHEN
REVISING

Subject:

Page:

Title:

Date:

Key Points:

Notes:

Summary:

SAY OUT
LOUD
WHEN
REVISING

THIS IS NOT A DOODLE PAGE 😊 DIAGRAMS/MIND-MAPS

Relates to Page: _____

Subject:

Page:

Title:

Date:

Key Points:

Notes:

Summary:

SAY OUT
LOUD
WHEN
REVISING

Subject:

Date:

Title:

Key Points:

Notes:

Summary:

SAY OUT
LOUD
WHEN
REVISING

Subject: _____

Page: _____

Title: _____

Date: _____

Key Points:

Notes:

Summary:

SAY OUT
LOUD
WHEN
REVISING

Relates to Page: _____

Subject:

Page:

Title:

Date:

Key Points:

Notes:

Summary:

SAY OUT
LOUD
WHEN
REVISING

Page:	Subject:
Date:	Title:

Key Points:

Notes:

Summary:

SAY OUT
LOUD
WHEN
REVISING

Subject:

Page:

Title:

Date:

Key Points:

Notes:

Summary:

SAY OUT
LOUD
WHEN
REVISING

THiS iS NOT A DOODLE PAGE :) DiAGRAMS/MiND-MAPS

Relates to Page: _____

Subject:

Page:

Title:

Date:

Key Points:

Notes:

Summary:

SAY OUT
LOUD
WHEN
REVISING

Page:	Subject:
Date:	Title:

Key Points:

Notes:

Summary:

SAY OUT
LOUD
WHEN
REVISING

Subject:

Page:

Title:

Date:

Key Points:

Notes:

Summary:

SAY OUT
LOUD
WHEN
REVISING

Relates to Page: _____

Subject:

Page:

Title:

Date:

Key Points:

Notes:

Summary:

SAY OUT
LOUD
WHEN
REVISING

Page:	Subject:
Date:	Title:

Key Points:

Notes:

Summary:

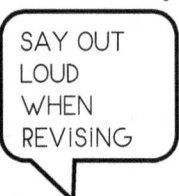

SAY OUT
LOUD
WHEN
REVISING

Subject:

Page:

Title:

Date:

Key Points:

Notes:

Summary:

SAY OUT
LOUD
WHEN
REVISING

Relates to Page: _____

Title:

Date:

Key Points:

Notes:

Summary:

SAY OUT
LOUD
WHEN
REVISING

Page:	Subject:
Date:	Title:

Key Points:

Notes:

Summary:

SAY OUT
LOUD
WHEN
REVISING

Subject:

Title: .

Date:

Key Points:

Notes:

Summary:

SAY OUT
LOUD
WHEN
REVISING

THiS iS NOT A DOODLE PAGE :) DiAGRAMS/MiND-MAPS

Relates to Page: _____

Subject:

Page:

Title:

Date:

Key Points:

Notes:

Summary:

SAY OUT
LOUD
WHEN
REVISING

Page: Subject:

Date: Title:

Key Points: Notes:

Summary:

SAY OUT
LOUD
WHEN
REVISING

Subject: Page:

Title: Date:

Key Points: Notes:

Summary:

SAY OUT
LOUD
WHEN
REVISING

THIS IS NOT A DOODLE PAGE 😊 DIAGRAMS/MIND-MAPS

Relates to Page: _____

Subject:

Page:

Title:

Date:

Key Points:

Notes:

Summary:

SAY OUT
LOUD
WHEN
REVISING

Page:	Subject:
Date:	Title:

Key Points:

Notes:

Summary:

SAY OUT
LOUD
WHEN
REVISING

Subject:

Page:

Title:

Date:

Key Points:

Notes:

Summary:

SAY OUT
LOUD
WHEN
REVISING

THiS iS NOT A DOODLE PAGE 😊 DiAGRAMS/MiND-MAPS

Relates to Page: _____

Subject:	Page:
Title:	Date:

Key Points:

Notes:

Summary:

SAY OUT
LOUD
WHEN
REVISING

Page:	Subject:
Date:	Title:

Key Points:

Notes:

Summary:

SAY OUT
LOUD
WHEN
REVISING

Subject: Page:

Title: Date:

Key Points:

Notes:

Summary:

SAY OUT
LOUD
WHEN
REVISING

Relates to Page: _____

Subject:

Page:

Title:

Date:

Key Points:

Notes:

Summary:

SAY OUT
LOUD
WHEN
REVISING

Page:	Subject:
Date:	Title:

Key Points:

Notes:

Summary:

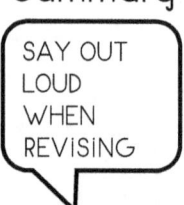
SAY OUT
LOUD
WHEN
REVISING

Subject:

Page:

Title:

Date:

Key Points:

Notes:

Summary:

SAY OUT
LOUD
WHEN
REVISING

THiS iS NOT A DOODLE PAGE 🙂 DiAGRAMS/MiND-MAPS

Relates to Page: _____

Subject:

Page:

Title:

Date:

Key Points:

Notes:

Summary:

SAY OUT
LOUD
WHEN
REVISING

Page:	Subject:
Date:	Title:

Key Points:

Notes:

Summary:

SAY OUT
LOUD
WHEN
REVISING

Subject:

Page:

Title:

Date:

Key Points:

Notes:

Summary:

SAY OUT
LOUD
WHEN
REVISING

THIS IS NOT A DOODLE PAGE :) DIAGRAMS/MIND-MAPS

Relates to Page: _____

Subject:

Page:

Title:

Date:

Key Points:

Notes:

Summary:

SAY OUT
LOUD
WHEN
REVISING

Page:	Subject:
Date:	Title:

Key Points:

Notes:

Summary:

SAY OUT
LOUD
WHEN
REVISING

Subject:

Page:

Title:

Date:

Key Points:

Notes:

Summary:

SAY OUT
LOUD
WHEN
REVISING

Relates to Page: _____

Subject:

Page:

Title:

Date:

Key Points:

Notes:

Summary:

SAY OUT
LOUD
WHEN
REVISING

Subject:

Date:

Title:

Key Points:

Notes:

Summary:

SAY OUT
LOUD
WHEN
REVISING

Subject:

Page:

Title:

Date:

Key Points:

Notes:

Summary:

SAY OUT
LOUD
WHEN
REVISING

Relates to Page: _____

Subject:

Page:

Title:

Date:

Key Points:

Notes:

Summary:

SAY OUT
LOUD
WHEN
REVISING

Subject:

Date:

Title:

Key Points:

Notes:

Summary:

SAY OUT
LOUD
WHEN
REVISING

Subject:

Page:

Title:

Date:

Key Points:

Notes:

Summary:

SAY OUT
LOUD
WHEN
REVISING

Relates to Page: _____

Subject:

Page:

Title:

Date:

Key Points:

Notes:

Summary:

SAY OUT
LOUD
WHEN
REVISING

Page:	Subject:
Date:	Title:

Key Points:

Notes:

Summary:

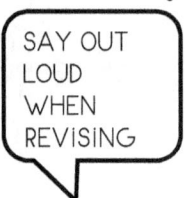

SAY OUT
LOUD
WHEN
REVISING

Subject:

Page:

Title:

Date:

Key Points:

Notes:

Summary:

SAY OUT
LOUD
WHEN
REVISING

Relates to Page: _____

Key Points:

Notes:

Page:	Subject:
Date:	Title:

Key Points:

Notes:

Summary:

SAY OUT
LOUD
WHEN
REVISING

Subject:

Page:

Title:

Date:

Key Points:

Notes:

Summary:

SAY OUT
LOUD
WHEN
REVISING

THiS iS NOT A DOODLE PAGE 😊 DiAGRAMS/MiND-MAPS

Relates to Page: _____

Subject:

Page:

Title:

Date:

Key Points:

Notes:

Summary:

SAY OUT
LOUD
WHEN
REVISING

Page:	Subject:
Date:	Title:

Key Points:

Notes:

Summary:

SAY OUT
LOUD
WHEN
REVISING

Subject:

Page:

Title:

Date:

Key Points:

Notes:

Summary:

SAY OUT
LOUD
WHEN
REVISING

Relates to Page: _____

Subject:

Page:

Title:

Date:

Key Points:

Notes:

Summary:

SAY OUT
LOUD
WHEN
REVISING

Page:	Subject:
Date:	Title:

Key Points:

Notes:

Summary:

SAY OUT
LOUD
WHEN
REVISING

Subject: Page:

Title: Date:

Key Points: Notes:

Summary:

SAY OUT
LOUD
WHEN
REVISING

Relates to Page: _____

Subject: Page:

Title: Date:

Key Points: Notes:

Summary:

SAY OUT
LOUD
WHEN
REVISING

Subject:

Title:

Key Points:

Notes:

Summary:

SAY OUT
LOUD
WHEN
REVISING

Subject: _____ Page: ____

Title: _____ Date: ____

Key Points:

Notes:

Summary:

SAY OUT
LOUD
WHEN
REVISING

Relates to Page: _____

Subject:

Page:

Title:

Date:

Key Points:

Notes:

Summary:

SAY OUT
LOUD
WHEN
REVISING

Page: Subject:

Date: Title:

Key Points: Notes:

Summary:

SAY OUT
LOUD
WHEN
REVISING

Subject:

Page:

Title:

Date:

Key Points:

Notes:

Summary:

SAY OUT
LOUD
WHEN
REVISING

Relates to Page: _____

NOTES

NOTES